TAKE A LETTER

or,
The Youthful Architect's
Epistolary Companion

SINCLAIR GAULDIE

DEDICATED
to
all youthful architects
of whatever age
and to
those
who correct their spelling, their punctuation,
their modes of address
and much, much more
and have no other monument
than the initials after the oblique.

First published in 1990 by The Royal Incorporation of Architects in Scotland,
15 Rutland Square, Edinburgh EH1 2BE

© Sinclair Gauldie

ISBN 1-873190-00-X

Printed by Stevenson (Printers) Ltd, Dundee

FOREWORD

*I cherish my father's copies of H B Creswell's classics; I shall cherish
Sinclair's classic. It made me laugh – pause – think – and laugh again.
Humour is the best mode for instruction – especially humour rooted
in reality. This is a book to instruct architects and other professionals
– and one, if given to one's more trusted clients, to increase understanding of an architect's cares and concerns.*

*Dundee has proved a wonderful stable for enterprise and wisdom –
in its architects and businessmen. Sinclair leads the field, steeped in
experience from fifty years' practice, tempered by the heat and fury
of RIAS Practice Committee and matured by some famous
arbitrations.*

*He exhibits to perfection in this book the four ingredients essential to
a happy life:– Commonsense, prudence, pride in his profession and a
sense of the ridiculous. I am privileged to be able to commend it to his
readers.*

John D Spencely
President RIAS
Summer 1990

CONTENTS

AUTHOR'S NOTE

This book is not intended simply for amusement. Indeed such giggles as it contains are necessary means to a serious instructional end.

I was convinced quite early in life, by the example of a truly memorable and civilised schoolmaster, that laughter was far superior to thrashing or sarcasm as a means of lodging lessons in the memory. I had not forgotten that example when the time came for me to earn a welcome spare-time guinea by lecturing on professional practice to architectural students and the fact that they remained awake (one of the most wide-awake was later to become President of the RIBA) must prove something.

It was in those days that I realised how little a full-time architectural student was taught of the difficult and dangerous art of correspondence. In the remote past, when architects were trained by a four or five years' apprenticeship, it was an incurious apprentice indeed who did not pick up something of that art through the daily traffic of the office, by the same process of osmosis (or, bluntly, eavesdropping) by which he acquired the art of the well-conducted telephone call and the polite but firm interview. I am not wholly convinced that the present two years of compressed office training, rather later in life, provide a true equivalent.

So my purpose here is to produce something roughly equivalent to the old-fashioned calf-bound "letter-book" where, in my father's apprentice days, the whole correspondence of a practice was copied day by day and which made available, to any apprentice who cared to sample it, a rich quarry of precedents to suit all occasions.

In this I am, of course, following in the hallowed footsteps of H B Creswell whose *Honeywood* books were by far the most palatable among the required reading of my own student years. So I have presumed to make my fictitious correspondent the son of his fictitious correspondent, and I trust that his genial ghost will take it as a tribute rather than a liberty.

I have to add that he and all the other characters in this book are indeed fictitious and no reference whatever to any real person, living or dead, is to be read into them.

INTRODUCTION

James Leslie Spinlove, FRIBA (1930–1988) – latterly senior partner in the architectural firm of Spinlove and Spinlove – was the only son of that firm's founder, James Spinlove (d. 1960) and his wife, Phyllis (née Brash) (d. 1975). The elder Spinlove is remembered, if at all, not so much for his buildings as for the extracts from his office correspondence which the late H B Creswell published in 1929 and 1930 as *The Honeywood File* and *The Honeywood Settlement*.

It was characteristic of the son to have left express instructions that when, as he put it, "the day comes for me to join Chris Wren and the boys in The Great Members' Bar In The Sky", no fulsome obituary should appear in any of the professional journals. Consequently the reader will search in vain for any formal reference to his passing.

In any event, the professional press would hardly have treated it as a prime news item, since Spinlove maintained, throughout his life, a profile so low as to be virtually concave. He was painfully aware that Nature never intended him to be an architect, and nothing in his career suggests that Nature was mistaken. He was plainly designed for success in the literary field, or in one of the gentler arts, such as book illustration, rather than in the rough and tumble of private architectural practice.

In particular, he inherited from his mother a sharpish way with words, and from his grandfather, Sir Leslie Brash, a very short fuse: both of these disabilities tended to show up in his correspondence. It was only after the second of the libel actions against him was settled out of court that his professional indemnity insurers persuaded him to adopt the method employed by Mark Twain – that is, to re-write every letter in more temperate and considered terms on the following day.

By pursuing this wise course, he maintained himself in honourable and profitable practice for the rest of his life. But (like Mark Twain) he could not bear to part with his first drafts and a whole trunkful of them came to light after his death. The following pages contain a selection from that archive, matched in each case by the re-draft as lodged in the correspondence files of Spinlove and Spinlove (now Spinlove, Spinlove and Spinlove) by whose permission they are reproduced.

There is a short editorial commentary on each letter which may be of interest to the serious student. These are printed as an appendix at the back of the book, where they will not obtrude upon the entertainment of the more frivolous reader.

M.D., Brogan's Brewery

Clerk of Works

D— Sir

Surprise, surprise!   Champagne Charlie Malagrowther
still alive! He must be pretty strapped for a
reference when he gives you my name — it must be
about 8 years since he last worked with us, and
our relationship was wearing a trifle thin by that
time. An architect likes to feel that the Clerk of
Works is sober within working hours. If not cold
sober, at least sober enough to get up on the scaffold
& have a look-see — which Charlie was not all that
keen upon, especially after about 3 p.m. and on
cold winter days, which he preferred to spend in
his hut, writing-up the state of the weather, the
number of men on site etc. in his immaculate
copperplate.

I can't think of any more fitting final chapter
to his career than this extension to your brewery
— his spiritual home, one might say.

But to be fair — for all I know, he may have pulled
his socks up & taken the cure, & certainly he had been
a first-class Clerk of Works at one time. He had looked
after some very high-class contracts in the 60's and
knew the building trade from back to front. When
he chose to do so, he could really make his presence
felt, but without causing disastrous confrontations
on site.

I really don't know what to say about Charlie.
It's a pity he didn't refer you to somebody with
more recent experience of working with him — but maybe
that's a bad sign. He'd probably be O.K. with a
careful architect who recognised his weak points &
appreciated the good ones: could be disastrous with
the type who never visits the site & leaves it all to the
C. of. W.   More than that, I can't honestly say

y—f—

J.S.

CONFIDENTIAL

The Managing Director
Brogans Barset Beers Ltd.
Barchester **BX21 3LM**

Dear Sir

Clerk of Works
Mr Malachi Charles Malagrowther

Thank you for your letter of 15 September asking for a reference on
Mr Malagrowther, who has applied for the post of Clerk of Works on
the extension to your brewery.

It is some eight years since we worked with Mr Malagrowther and we
have had no contact with him since then. We were under the impression
that he had retired.

He acted as Clerk of Works for two contracts for which we were architects,
one of £450,740 and the other of £612,738. Both were works of traditional
construction requiring a good standard of finish: neither had an
unusually high element of electrical/mechanical services.

He was invariably courteous, helpful and anxious to please, and fully
recognised his position as inspector on behalf of the architect while
never presuming upon it or exceeding his authority. He kept immaculate
records and made prompt weekly returns of such matters as weather,
manpower and visitors. He was not latterly as physically active in his
site inspections as a younger man might have been, but at that time his
health could have been better.

He had the considerable advantage of long experience of inspecting the
work of the traditional building trades. He did however rely quite
substantially on the presence and backing of the architect: in our case
we made site visits at least once a week and often more frequently.

As far as we know, he is not a member of the Institute of Clerks of Works.

If you require further information, perhaps you would be good enough to
telephone the writer.

Yours faithfully

JAMES L SPINLOVE

Secretary
Barchester Chamber of Commerce

Sir,
        You are an impudent <u>liar</u>.

Our subscription was paid long ago.
Kindly get your books put into some
kind of decent order, and stop bothering
us with these fatuous x unnecessary
reminders.
                    yours

The Director
Barchester Chamber of Commerce
Barchester **BX1 1MS**

Dear Sir

Annual Subscription
_____

With reference to your letter of 27 February, the cheque in payment of
our subscription was cleared by your bank on 15 January as you will see
from the enclosed photocopy.

In order to avoid further misunderstandings of this kind, we shall
arrange to make this payment in future years by standing order or
direct debit.

Yours faithfully

SPINLOVE & SPINLOVE

Mrs Wanda Rose Thynnges
Dear Wanda   "High Jinx"
   After your 4th. phone call, my secretary said:
"She's one of those belles that now & then rings."
My staff are all agog to know what you meant by
"a chat about some of the little extras before Quintin
gets back from his business trip to Bangkok." I
suppose the extras you mean are the items which
I warned you would all show up in the final valuation,
but after your behaviour at the housewarming party,
I wonder... To put it bluntly, I'm not crossing your
threshold without one of my minders in tow.
   Moneywise, Cypher & I have done our best to keep
you in the picture, but, let's face it, you and Quintin
did go on clocking-up extras like there was no
tomorrow & now it is tomorrow & all the sweet talk
imaginable won't wish them away. The contractor
has his rights just as you have yours, & I have
to see both of you fairly treated. By the way,
don't invite young Mr. Grigblay round for one
of your little chats- he's not quite the oldfashioned
chap his grandfather was, & you could get more
than you bargained for - and nothing knocked off
the bill.
   Leave it with Joe Cypher & me to sort out—
we'll discuss it with you and Quintin when
Q. gets back.
                    yours ever
                              JS.

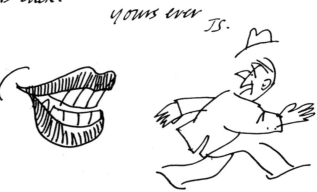

Mrs Q. St.J. Thynnges
"High Jinx"
Nr. Barchester **BX3 1FT**

Dear Mrs Thynnges

"High Jinx"
_____

I am sorry I was not available when you telephoned - I have had to be
away from the office a great deal lately on country business.

I share your concern for the outcome of the final valuation. As with
all new-build houses, not everything can be foreseen at the outset and
when the clients themselves possess creative imaginations, all sorts of
irresistible refinements do come to mind in the course of building -
and in the end of the day have to paid for under the terms of the building
contract. Fortunately the contract for your house was let to a reputable
and old established firm (in fact the people who built my own grandfather's
house, and who are still a family concern) and you need have no fear that
they will seek to take undue advantage of the numerous variations. In
any event, Mr Cypher is a very experienced and conscientious quantity
surveyor and can be relied upon to make sure that, while Grigblay is
entitled to his pound of flesh, he does not draw blood with it.

I am asking Mr Cypher to prepare an analysis of the final account which
will show in easily-understood terms where the money has gone and who
ordered what. Once he has done so, the four of us can get together
over it and sort out any queries. I think this exercise had better wait
until your husband comes back from the East, since you and he are both
equal signatories to the contract and so Mr Cypher and myself have to be
accountable to you jointly.

I expect you will think the tone of this letter rather formal, but I can
assure you from experience that a building contract - like a marriage one -
is not to be entered upon "unadvisedly, lightly or wantonly but discreetly
advisedly and soberly" and likewise the final winding-up of such a contract
has to be treated as quite a serious affair.

Kind regards.

Yours sincerely

Joe Cypher.
Dear Joe   "High Jinx"

Help! Wanda T. has been phoning relentlessly,
wanting a "chat about the little extras". <u>Little</u>!!
With her fantasies! And all that "Let's not spoil
the ship, old boy" stuff from himself!!

  I've been suspecting lately that they've been
expecting W's. dear old dad to pick up the tabs all
along & when the day of reckoning comes and he
gets a look at your final valuation, he'll pull the
plug on the pair of them. That's my guess anyway,
& let's <u>not</u> you & me be the human sacrifice at
that point.

  Let's face it, maybe you or I should have warned
them earlier that they'd put the skids under
the original cost-plan: but your delays —and, let's
not mince words— slaphappy optimism in the updating
of it didn't help any! For my part, I'd assumed
that, like most of your professional brethren, you'd
padded out the Bills of Quantities with so many
concealed "contingencies" (? the rock-cutting? the
provisional plumbing for the Jacuzzi?) that the
overall position was well in hand. Not so, I
can see from your draft report.

  <u>Tear it up!</u> Remember the old saying "If you
don't like the message, shoot the messenger"—
probably the Thynnge family motto. Let's have the
blame pinned where it belongs— on the bosoms of
dear Quintin & darling Wanda, <u>not</u> on ours. Bear
in mind that they made all the agreements &
contracts jointly, so neither of them can disown the
other's instructions: just about the only bit of
good luck we've had on this so-aptly named job.

  And let's go over the figures together <u>before</u>
the happy couple get anywhere near them, OK?
                              Yours Jim

Messrs J & J Cypher FFRICS
Chartered Quantity Surveyors
45 Market Street
Barchester **BX1 1MS**

Dear Sirs

"High Jinx"
Mr & Mrs Q St.J. Thynnges

It would be advisable to have a fairly early meeting with our clients
in order to explain to them the make-up of the final account and, in
particular, the reasons for the variations.

We would therefore suggest that you prepare a financial statement which
will show quite clearly - (e.g. as one column for additions and another
for deductions) - the effect of the several V.O.s. In each case, the
V.O. should be identified as :

　　originating from site emergency
　　　　"　　　　　" 　correction of billed quantity
　　　　"　　　　　" 　consultant structural engineer's variation
　　　　"　　　　　" 　consultant heating engineer's variation
　　　　"　　　　　" 　architect's instruction initiated by Mr Thynnge
　　　　"　　　　　" 　architect's instruction initiated by Mrs Thynnge
　　　　"　　　　　" 　other A.I.s.

It will of course be necessary for Mr Joseph Cypher to go over this
statement with us in draft before it is presented to our clients. We
understand that Mr Thynnge is abroad on business and since all agreements
have been made jointly by himself and Mrs Thynnge, it would clearly be
unwise to make any explanations until both can be present.

Yours faithfully

SPINLOVE & SPINLOVE

Barchester Brokers
D—S—   our P.I. Insurance

For years, I have restrained myself from comment
on the daft questions you ask at each renewal.
No Longer—

Question 7. I suppose you want us to divide our
work Into these "building types" so that underwriters
can guess the risk, but what imbecile devised the
categories? - e.g. "High-rise" - High-rise *what*?
"Government Buildings" — what do we do about high-rise
Government Buildings (we should be so lucky!) And
"Cathedrals" !! - if the underwriters employed real
statisticians instead of Hooray Henries, they would
know that the chance of a brand-new cathedral figuring
in an architect's workload in this year of grace is ZERO.

Question 10. How do you suppose we can "ensure"
anything about the business methods of consulting
engineers? Half the time, they are wished on us
by the client on the "Buggins's Turn" principle. When
we do have any choice, we don't pick cowboys.

Question 12 Some of our fee income comes from
providing services to Grigblay & Son (Builders) Ltd.
They have never built a duff house yet, & are not
Likely to do so: our involvement goes no further
than house-type designs & layouts. We are not
called-on to supervise or certify, so the work does
not show up in the figures for "work certified"
but only in those for "fees received"

What do you want to know the fees *for*, anyway?
So you can work out how big a premium you
can screw us for ??

Your incredibly complicated & inept Proposal
Form is returned herewith — completed and signed.
Thank God it comes but once a year.

                              y—t— JS

Barchester Brokers Ltd.
3 High Street
Barchester **BX1 1MS**

Dear Sirs

Professional Indemnity Insurance
Policy No. XYZ/00356/725/J

We return herewith the signed proposal form for the renewal of our indemnity
cover and would ask you to note the following points.

Question 7 We have assumed that "high-rise" means "in excess of 5 storeys",
that "Government Buildings" are buildings commissioned directly by Government
Departments and that these two terms are mutually exclusive. If we are
mistaken, please clarify.

Question 10 Where consultants are appointed by the client, we advise both
parties to define their relationship by a formal contract. They normally follow
this advice but we cannot "ensure" that they do so. We rarely engage consultants
on our own account. When we do, it is normally only for isolated "one-off"
items of advice: the consultants so engaged are normally well-known to us
and accept that they are expected to indemnify us.

Question 12   Our fees for the past year included £12,470 for professional
services provided to a local builder who is a member of the NHBC. These fees
were for type-plans and housing layouts: no supervision was undertaken and
the building firm itself was the client. Consequently we are not called upon
to certify the cost of the building work as executed, nor do we have any
accurate figures for it: sometimes the project goes no further than the sketch
stage.   Obviously this part of our workload is not reflected in the figures
for "work certified".

Yours faithfully

SPINLOVE & SPINLOVE

Cal McGurk —
Dear Mr. McGurk.   "McG's Motor Mecca"

When I saw your photograph in the local rag's
report of the Caledonian Society's Burns Supper —
- all got up in your tribal gear and apparently
about to plunge a claymore, or dirk, or whatever
into the heart of this harmless, inoffensive haggis —
I was suddenly reminded of a line written by
the aforesaid National Bard. If I mistake not,
he went on record to the effect that —
"It's guid to be honest and true."
In spite of your nefarious trade, I'm sure
you must have some desire to pass yourself
off as 'honest & true', if only in the eyes of the
various moneylenders whose plastic I see you
flashing around in the more broadminded
eateries and niteries of this fair city. So
let's see you unzip your sporran & come
across with my long-delayed fee. - Otherwise,
I'll have the heavies on you.
                    Yours aye - J.S.

Mr Caliban McGurk
"Bide-a-Wee"
Chantry Avenue
Barchester **BX1 3LM**

Dear Sir

McGurk's Motor Mecca

We are writing to your home since previous communications to your
business premises at Slaughterhouse Lane have been returned marked
"Not Known at this Address".

We refer to our four previous reminders that we have not received
payment of our fee – originally rendered more than two years ago –
for successfully negotiating the change of use of your property
from a disused abattoir to a used-car mart.

These reminders seem to have been ignored and, while we appreciate
that you may well be having your own cash-flow problems, we must
point out that we cannot extend credit indefinitely. Consequently
we must ask you to let us have your remittance within fourteen
days hereof, as otherwise we shall be obliged to put this debt
into the hands of our agents for collection.

Yours faithfully

SPINLOVE & SPINLOVE

Riddoppo Ltd.

Dear Sirs,

In reply to your effusion of All Fools' Day, the answer is NO

yours   Sgs.

Mr Spinlove thanks you for your
letter of 1st April inviting him
to the Buffet Luncheon and
demonstration of "New Riddoppo"
exterior wall treatment but
regrets that he is not in a
position to attend.

SPINLOVE & SPINLOVE

Sir Midas Hyphen-Hyphen
Dear Sir Midas,   St. Walpurgis School

Is there no end to your whingeing? I had a feeling, at last week's Building Committee, that I'd soon be on the receiving end of one of your lectures on how to do my job, but this one is the richest yet.

Just because you're the "anonymous" donor, (that's a good one, after all the winks & nudges) of the cash for the new chapel does _not_ make you automatically an authority on architecture, or any other damn thing apart from Money. Still less does it qualify you to question my decision on such a fine point as the correct choice of timber for the panelling.

I do understand your wish for a final result as close to perfection as can reasonably be expected, but I don't understand your fear that people would blame _you_ if English oak should turn out to be "rather too robust" a timber for a chapel for young ladies". If there is any blame going, it has to fall on _me_. I am the Architect, and you are only a Glorified Sharepusher.

Henceforth, be silent. Your job is to sign the cheques — just stick to it.

                    yours   JS

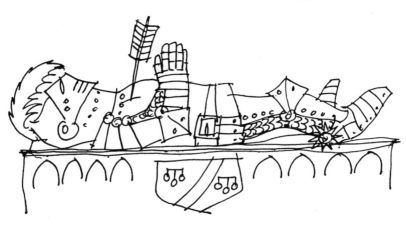

Sir Midas Hyphen-Hyphen
Upper Crust
Barsetshire **BX5 4BD**

Dear Sir Midas

St Walpurga's School for Girls : New Chapel

Your comments on my choice of wood for the chapel panelling have given
me much thought, and I think they deserve a considered answer: I hope
you will not find this too technical or boring.

Each of the panels is made up of short boards, joined together with
bars (called ledges") on the back, and fixed to the framing behind in
such a way that they can move according to shifts in temperature and/or
humidity, without cracking. The sizes of the panels are related
aesthetically to the length and height of the wall – if too small or
too large, they would distort the "scale" of the chapel in the eye
of the observer and spoil the whole effect.

Similarly, the profile of the boards comprising the panels (by which we
are trying to capture the effect of mediaeval "linenfold" panelling
within the sort of cost which is acceptable in this modern age) has to
be related to the scale of the panel, so as to be neither too flat and
insignificant, or too robust and coarse. Either way, the overall effect
would be ruined.

And finally, the texture and grain of the timber itself has to be related
to the scale of the profile of the boards. A more "feminine" timber –
such as the sycamore, or even Japanese Oak, which you were kind enough
to suggest – while very elegant indeed in itself would, in the context
of the scale of the boards, of the panels and of the room, lose its
quality and become rather insignificant. Hence my choice of the more
robust timber which although perhaps decidedly masculine in character
in the sample which I showed to the committee will, I assure you, appear
perfectly in character within the context of the chapel as a whole.

I hope I have made my decision clear, although these points of aesthetics
are always very difficult to resolve, even between professional designers.
If you feel that further explanation is required, please do not hesitate
to call upon me at any time.

Kind regards.

Yours sincerely

Peregrine Hyphen-Hyphen
Barchester Antiques.

Insolent Puppy —

You have the infernal cheek to suggest that
we are in some way to blame for the roof-leaks
in the annexe to your tatty junk-shop. You quote
some self-styled "building surveyor" (name and
qualifications not stated) as putting these down
to inadequacy in the design of the roof to withstand
snow load.

Come off it! This is mischievous & libellous
nonsense. Let me remind you that, when we designed
the annexe 5 years ago, you wouldn't pay for the
engagement of an independent structural engineer.
Since our insurers go all faint & trembly at the
idea of our doing these piddling calculations
ourselves, the roof-trusses were designed in-house
by the very competent firm who fabricated and
erected them, and they passed Building Control
without question.

Your steelwork has clearly become distorted by
some moron anchoring heavy lifting tackle to
the bottom boom of one of the trusses. No
doubt this is because you are using the annexe
as a garage for antique vehicles, instead of as
the store for _objets d'art_ which you originally
commissioned. There is one hell of a difference
between shifting china dogs from the escritoire
to the sideboard & whipping the engine out of a
1924 Albion truck. Get lost.

JS

24

FOR THE ATTENTION OF MR PEREGRINE HYPHEN-HYPHEN

Barchester Antiques Ltd.
Green Ginger Lane
Barchester BX1 3LM

Dear Sirs

We have received your letter of 15 June in which you ask us to
reimburse you for the repairs to the roof of your annexe.

We note that you have not seen fit to identify the surveyor
to whose report you refer, nor to send us a copy of it.

In our opinion, the deformation, which occurs in one truss only,
could not have resulted from any inadequacy of the steelwork to
withstand snow load. The roof trusses were correctly designed
to meet your instructions as to the purpose for which the building
was intended. Consequently we wholly repudiate any suggestion of
failure of professional duty on our part.

Yours faithfully

SPINLOVE & SPINLOVE

Barchester Brokers.

D— S—

Our Professional Indemnity Insce.
Barchester Antiques

We enclose copies of correspondence with this one-time client.

We are treating the chinless wonder with the contempt which he deserves — this is nothing but an impudent attempt to sting us for the cost of repairing a roof which his own bone-headed muscle-man has knackered.

Y—F—   S&S

Barchester Brokers Ltd.
3 High Street
Barchester **BX1 1MS**

Dear Sirs

Professional Indemnity Policy No. XYZ/00356/725/J

As required by the conditions of our policy, we enclose copies of the
exchange of correspondence between Mr Peregrine Hyphen-Hyphen and ourselves
regarding an alleged failure of roof trusses, which he apparently believes
to be due to some breach of professional duty on our part.

As you will notice, we have wholly repudiated any such suggestion and we
think it unlikely that he will pursue the claim further.

Yours faithfully

SPINLOVE & SPINLOVE

Bill Sikes
"The Vandal's Arms"

Aha!   Lounge Bar

So one of your regulars is "a practical chimney-sweep," is he? I have yet to meet a theoretical chimney-sweep, but I seem to recall that Oxford runs a course called Modern Grates (ha! ha!) so anything goes, these days.

If you must write down this man's advice, please use decent paper, not the backside of one of your vile bar-lunch menus. Still, that's just about the treatment it deserves.

I am not, as you seem to suspect, trying to sabotage your dream of a "genuine open fire with ingle-nook" in the lounge bar — just trying to get you to face the facts, viz. that the only practicable place for it would involve running a flue up your neighbour's gable & he won't allow it. The wall suggested by your sweep won't do, as IT HAS A BLOODY GREAT STEEL GIRDER IN THE MIDDLE OF IT. How do I know? Because my old man put it there in 1939.

Stop listening to every Thomas, Richard & Henry who drops in for a pint — your architect has at least enough common sense to check the facts before he runs off at the mouth. If you don't believe me, just bash the wall down and see.

Why not just put in a fake flickering fire — it would go nicely with the fake rafters, the fake leather & the fake candles which the previous licensee put in. Granted, your sweep couldn't spit in it, but what's he doing in the lounge bar anyway?

And don't call me "Jimmy"
                        yours JS

William Sikes Esq.
The Vandals Arms
Malt Street
Barchester **BX1 1MS**

Dear Mr Sikes

Proposed Alterations to Lounge Bar

Thank you for your note giving me Mr Finnegan's advice on the location
of the fireplace.

While I appreciate his enthusiasm – and I must make it clear that I do
agree with you that a genuine open fire would be an asset – there is no
getting away from the fact that only two walls are free for this, and
one of them is ruled out by the adjoining owners' refusal to have a flue
rising up their gable above your roof.

The other would be eminently suitable, as your customer points out,
except for one thing which perhaps I did not make sufficiently clear
during our discussion. The alterations which were carried out in 1939,
and for which my late father was the architect, involved considerable
alterations in the area of that particular wall, including the insertion
of a deep steel girder in a position which would prevent a flue rising
up at any point along its length. This is clearly shown on our records
but if you are in doubt you could remove the panelling, when I think
you will find that the work was executed as shown on the 1939 plans.

Perhaps you should compromise and instal a reproduction fire which would
need no flue. Some of these are very realistic nowadays, and it would
suit the general decor which I believe you wish to remain unchanged.

I look forward to seeing you at the Rugby Club Old Crocks Get-together
next week.

Yours sincerely

SPINLOVE & SPINLOVE

Joe Cypher
Dear Joe,   "High Jinx"

Lucky you, to be on holiday — moustique, no doubt —
otherwise I'd have had your guts for garters. Hardly
had you gone when your sidekick, Gradgrind, was
on the blower, asking for an A.I. to cover the roofing of
the stable wing. Now he tells me — left out of the BQ's,
no less. Well, we can all make them, & I admit that in
times past you've covered for me (as I have for you), but
there <u>has</u> to be a limit, and this is it. Gradgrind
wants me to save your blushes by putting our name to
a bit of paper which not only is unnecessary but could
open the door to a rip-off by the contractor. NO WAY.
     If the Thynngses get their hands on the details
of your final measurement (which God forbid) and can
manage to decipher them (most unlikely!) and find
out that you omitted the stable roofing, then let the
blame lie where it falls — not, repeat NOT, on my doorstep.
If my chaps can find the time to <u>draw</u> the damn thing
properly, surely yours can find the time to bill it
properly.
     Too bad you should escape the dreaded barracuda
in the Caribbean to come back to letters like this one
— but life ain't all sunshine & Bacardi
                         yours
                              Jim

Messrs J & J Cypher FFRICS
Chartered Quantity Surveyors
45 Market Street
BARCHESTER   BX1 1MS

Dear Sirs
"High Jinx" : Mr & Mrs Q St.J. Thynnges
We refer to your Mr Gradgrind's telephone call this morning.

We wish to confirm our view that it is not necessary, and could well
be harmful to the interests of our mutual client, if we were to issue
a retrospective Architect's Instruction to cover the roof tiling on
the stable wing, which was apparently omitted from the contract bills.

This work is clearly shown on the contract drawings, we have not
amended our requirements in any particular and the work has, in fact,
been carried out in accordance with these drawings and completed
without any demur or query on the part of the contractor. There is
therefore no occasion for us to issue any further instruction.

The contractor is undoubtedly entitled to payment for the additional
tiling, but only as a variation to which he is automatically entitled
under the terms of the contract, as arising from an error in the
contract bills. To treat this variation other than in strict accordance
with that contract condition would, in our opinion, open the door to
quite unjustifiable claims.

We should be glad to discuss this with Mr Joseph Cypher on his return
from holiday.

Yours faithfully

SPINLOVE & SPINLOVE

The C.P.O.
Barchester D.C.

Dear George,   St. Walpurgis School Chapel

I know that 'all beauty is in the eye of the beholder', but this is ridiculous.

Your understrapper, Mr. A. Trollope, has the nerve to warn me that our submission doesn't meet his aesthetic standards & won't be recommended to your committee. Well...I hope you don't propose to insult their intelligence—frail though it is— with the kind of balderdash Trollope has dished out to me. His objection seems to be that our design "is not in keeping" with the existing building, which he describes as "English Perpendicular". God knows why he should malign one of the purest Gothic modes by confusing it with the vile pseudo-Venetian of the 1872 building - if your flunkeys must dabble in phoney historicism, they could at least get their facts right.

Since it's manifestly impossible to replicate that costly rubbish, this requirement would kill off any future extension to the school. I know one Governor who would willingly tear you apart with his bare hands if you pushed your committee into that decision.

Let me point out that harmony & uniformity are two different things—surely my grandfather & I could meet harmoniously without my wearing his cast-off clothes? Volumes have been written on this topic, but evidently not read by Mr. Trollope, who is probably more conversant with "land-use studies."

It's probably too late to change his reading habits. —Why not give him early retirement, and let him get on with something harmless —Like finishing one of those half-written novels which everyone knows he has in his desk drawer.   Yours   Tim

Up the airy mountain, Down the rushy glen, We dare not go a-hunting for fear of little men

The Chief Planning Officer
Barchester District Council
BARCHESTER   BX1 1MS

Dear Sir

Extension to St Walpurgis School for Girls

We refer to the telephone call received this morning from your
assistant, Mr Trollope, regarding our submission for approval of
the above proposals.

I gather that your Department is not disposed to support this
application, on the grounds that the external appearance of the
addition would not be in conformity with "the style of the original
building". Obviously this is a matter of opinion and, if I may say
so, my own opinion as an architect of many years' standing is not one
which your committee should lightly disregard;especially as
Mr Trollope's views, if literally interpreted, would effectively
preclude any extension whatever to the school. I need hardly enlarge
on the probable reaction of the large number of influential people in
the country who have its interests very much at heart.

I need hardly add that the attempt to create something which, without
replicating the details of the original, is sympathetic to its
character is a delicate exercise whose essential quality perhaps
cannot be fully judged from drawings of the kind which are normally
submitted for planning approval. Perhaps Mr Trollope would take a
different view if I had the opportunity of amplifying the proposals
in discussion. In any such discussion I would hope to give conclusive
arguments in favour of our solution,and in view of his personal interest
as Chairman of the School's Building Committee it might well be that
Sir Midas Hyphen-Hyphen would wish to be present also.

Please suggest a date and time which would be convenient.

Yours faithfully

JAMES L SPINLOVE

Flabbergast Sprinhcock & Stryver

Dear Sirs.

Bickerstaffe & BKS Punch-up

Well, it had to come my way sooner or later, given my notoriety as a man of honour & experience.

I'm glad that they picked somebody answering to that description in their own backyard (however slight — in my case, non-existent- his expertise in the law) and didn't go inviting a nominee from some impersonal body, whose trips down from London or wherever could cost them plenty. According to your Mr. Carton (although he phoned just after lunch & could have been a little confused) it is simply a matter of a disagreement among honest men, not among crooks who are trying to squeeze the last drop of blood out of the small print.

As such, they will be looking for a quick & inexpensive settlement, not a field-day for lawyers. If there absolutely _must_ be a formal hearing, with legal eagles hired by each side to peck at the other, I am going to need an eagle of my own to keep me right on procedural matters (eg. when to produce the red card) & this will cost a packet on top of my own (not inconsiderable) fee. But it does look as if I can sort it all out on a "documents only" basis at much less expense.

Once I know my exact (& I mean exact) terms of reference, I shall call a meeting with the solicitors for both sides so that the parties' heads can be banged together as painlessly as possible.

Yours faithfully,
J—S—

Messrs Flabbergast, Spatchcock and Stryver
Solicitors
12a Goblin Market
BARCHESTER   BX1 2MS

Dear Sirs

Proposed Arbitration
Mr Isaac Bickerstaff
        and
Barchester Kitchen Studio Ltd.

I refer to my telephone conversation yesterday with your Mr Sydney
Carton, regarding the dispute upon which the parties wish me to arbitrate.
I confirm that I have no relationship with either party which would
preclude my acting in that capacity, and that I am prepared to accept
nomination subject to my approval of the terms of the arbitration
agreement referring the dispute to me.

I assume that the parties wish to have their dispute settled as
expeditously and inexpensively as possible. It may be that I can
arrive at a decision on the basis of documents only: this would obviate
the need for a formal hearing which in itself involves a considerable
outlay on legal fees, not least those of the clerk and legal adviser
whom I should require to sit with me.

I therefore propose to state dates by which the parties must provide
me with the Points of Claim and with the Defence and Counterclaim, after
which I shall state further dates for the filing of further and better
particulars and for the reply to the counterclaim (if any), for the
discovery and inspection of documents and the filing of an agreed bundle
of numbered documents.

On the basis of these submissions, I shall make an interlocutory award
and invite representations upon it from the parties. These representations
may include a request for a hearing. If either party makes such a request
I shall arrange a date and place for that hearing and sit with an
independent legal adviser of my choice. If no such request is made I
shall, after considering the parties' representations, make my final award.
Once I have issued my formal acceptance of the reference I shall arrange
a meeting with the solicitors for the parties to discuss procedural details.
Yours faithfully

The Editor
"The Barsetshire Leader"

Sir,
    I was distressed by your report of remarks passed
at the AGM of the "Friends of Barsetshire" regarding
the design for the chapel at St. Walpurgis' School.
    I quite understand Mr. Peregrine Hyphen-Hyphen's
concern for the "architectural integrity" of the 1872 building,
which, if not to everyone's taste, is at least an interesting
example of historical pastiche. No doubt the surest way
of obviating criticism would have been to replicate
its style exactly. But, despite the great generosity of an
anonymous benefactor, the resources for such an
exercise simply do not exist. I need only point to the
enormous difficulty in finding adequately expert
stonemasons for the repairs to our own cathedral here.
    Surely any responsible architect must " cut the coat
according to the cloth", and seek a mode of expression
which, while not inharmonious, is necessarily somewhat
less, shall we say, exuberant than the style of the old
building. and, at the same time, is perhaps rather less
likely to give offence than the outright Miesian
approach advocated by Dr. Aardvark.
    I would not claim that my own solution is so
right as to be inevitable - far from it. But I would
remind your readers of the placard which Oscar Wilde
saw on a piano in his hotel in Leadville, Nevada:-
    " PLEASE DO NOT SHOOT THE PIANIST. HE IS DOING HIS BEST"
                        yours
                        James L. Spinlove

The Editor
"The Barsetshire Leader"
2 Printinghouse Court
BARCHESTER BX1 2GM

Sir

It is not my habit to defend myself in the correspondence columns of
the press, but your report of the intemperate attack delivered by the
"Friends of Barsetshire" upon my design for the St Walpurgis School
chapel compels me to do so.

St Walpurgis was built in 1872 as a country mansion for a self-made
millionaire. As such, it embodies certain aspirations peculiar to its
period, and expresses them in an architectural language which is not
ours. Precisely why the original architect adopted the Venetian Gothic
idiom is not known. It is incontestable, however, that this style is
wholly inappropriate to a non-denominational chapel for a girls' school
in Barsetshire in the latter part of the twentieth century. Equally,
I reject the view, expressed by one of the speakers, that "something
uncompromisingly modern - say in the style of Mies van der Rohe" would
be preferable. The purpose of this building would not be well-served
either by an exercise in sterile antiquarianism or by facile
exhibitionism. If a place of worship should exemplify anything at this
point in time it must surely be the injunction to "love thy neighbour",
disregard of which will self-evidently lead to the extinction of life
on this planet. Loving your neighbour does not mean imitating your
neighbour nor upstaging him but coexisting with him peaceably. The way
to do this in architecture is to aim at a harmony of proportion in the
disposition of mass and space and a harmony of texture and colour, all
of which can be achieved - if the architect exercises care - without
slavish imitation.

It may well be that I have not succeeded as well as I would have wished,
but to describe my proposals as "historically inappropriate" or "wishy-
washy" is singularly imperceptive. If this is the best the "Friends of
Barsetshire" can do, then God help Barsetshire.

Yours

JAMES L SPINLOVE

Grigblay

"High Jinx"

you plausible rogue!

Your impudence compels admiration. Yes, the roof-tiling on the stable was left out of the BQ's. Yes, this entitles you to payment for extra tiling. Yes, your tilers had to spend more time than you had programmed for - if, like a fool, you programmed from the Bills without looking at our drawings. But you know very well that the Bills are not prepared (at the client's expense) just to save you the trouble of using your loaf & appraising the job properly. And you know perfectly well that no A.I. is needed to correct a billing error of this kind: & you are not going to get one.

I see your little game - you over-ran by 4 weeks & now you want a retrospective extension of time which will not only wipe out your delay, but also reimburse you for a fictitious "direct loss and expense". Over my dead body, Grigblay lad - to quote the old Barsetshire saying "I be too old a bird to be took wi' a fistful o' chaff" and I am not in the business of handing out our clients' money to smart alecks.

Go to hell.

J.L. Spinlove

PS. Old grandpa Grigblay must be turning in his grave.

Grigblay Builders Ltd.
12/14 Appleyard Road
BARCHESTER BX1 1DQ

Dear Sirs

Mr and Mrs Q. St. J. Thynnges
"High Jinx"

We refer to your letter of 29 April claiming an extension of time
on the grounds of delayed architect's instructions for the additional
roof tiling to the stable.

We would point out that:

(a)   No such AI is required, since the correction of an error
      in billed quantities automatically constitutes a variation.

(b)   Your request is, in any case, out of order, not having been
      made at the proper time in the proper manner.

(c)   There is no evidence that the additional tiling caused delay
      to your overall programme. If, as you say, you had to place
      an additional order for materials, it may have been because
      you originally ordered from the bills without reference to
      the drawings: you must be well aware of the impropriety of
      that procedure.

We therefore reject your request for an extension of time on the grounds
put forward and we shall maintain our advice to our client that you are
liable for the liquidated and ascertained damages at the contractual
rate in respect of the four weeks by which the contract completion date
has been over-run.

If you wish to refer this question to arbitration, we should be glad of
early notification.

Yours faithfully

SPINLOVE & SPINLOVE

Sir Midas Hyphen-Hyphen.

Dear Scrooge   Barsetshire Building Society

As Shakespeare put it "Who would have thought the old man had so much blood in him?" Frankly, my first impression of you was indeed of a bloodless money-machine, but now you oblige me to re-think. Somewhere in those gloomy depths there lurks, after all, a human being who is prepared to do his fellow-man a bit of good without looking for a rake-off.

As a matter of fact, I thought I had noticed twinkles of emergent humanity in those reptilian eyes of yours during our more recent dealings, & I must admit that your backing in the planning row over the chapel was all that I could have wished. Maybe contact with my genial & cultured personality has awakened the immortal soul which has been lying dormant beneath the moneybags. Maybe not. There could be a catch somewhere, which I probably won't see until it's too late.

Or maybe I'm just getting cynical. Anyway, thanks a lot for the Building Society recommendation — we could use the work.

Ever thine

Tim Spinlove

Sir Midas Hyphen-Hyphen
Upper Crust
Barsetshire BX5 4BD

Dear Sir Midas

I have just heard from Mr Parbuckle of the Barsetshire Building
Society that their Board has confirmed our appointment as architects
for the new Headquarters building, and that this is a direct result
of your own recommendation.

I need hardly say that we welcome the opportunity of tackling this
important project, not least because of the interesting problem
presented by its site between the Clothiers' Hall and Vandals' Arms.
As these are both listed buildings, we must no doubt expect reference
to the Royal Fine Art Commission. This in itself will be an interesting
experience and a challenge which we welcome.

On a purely personal note, I would like to think that this recommendation
is a reflection of a rapport between us which has been steadily growing
since the inception of the St Walpurgis' School project, which could
hardly have got off the ground without your support and influence and,
not least, your understanding of the architect's point of view.

With kind regards to yourself and Lady Hyphen-Hyphen.

Yours sincerely

JAMES SPINLOVE

Quintin Thynnges
Dear Quintin   "High Jinx"
     Your letter said just what I thought it would.
Given your nit-picking instincts, it was hardly to
be expected that Joe Cypher's booboo wouldn't come
to light. I thought he owned-up very honestly — but
don't try hammering him for the money : after all,
you do _have_ the roof.
     About ~~the~~ Final Certificate — final is final is _final_
It means that, as far as our inspections show, Grigblay
has done what he contracted to do, & you'd better pay up.
     So there are marks on the bath enamel - I did eventually
find them, with the help of a large and powerful magnifying
glass. There's no way of proving they were made by G's
men before hand-over. Wanda admits that neither of
you saw them until that old hag of a mother of hers
"discovered" them 7 months later. I suppose you do
bathe several times in 7 months? I bet you'd have
seen them if they were there when you moved in —
you picked every other nit you could think of, down
to trying the fit of the doors with an engineer's
feeler-gauge.
     ~~And~~ pay our fee. I'm not impressed by the
argument that you should get a bit off because Wanda
suffers from headaches & insomnia on account of the
master-bedroom being planned across a prehistoric
ley-line running from Much Mumping to Glastonbury.
Her symptoms are due to being married to a ghastly
bore & swilling too much gin.
                         Come off it!
                              James

Quintin St. J. Thynnges
"High Jinx"
Nr. BARCHESTER

Dear Quintin   ·

"High Jinx"

Thank you for your letter of the 18th confirming your telephone call.

I fully understand your disappointment that the amount of the final
account, in spite of all our efforts, exceeded the tender figure, even
although only by £273. As Cypher explained, this was more than
accounted for by the regrettable error in the billing of the stable
roof which did not come to light until it was too late to make counter-
balancing amendments.

The Final Certificate does not debar you for recovering damages against
Grigblay if, at some time in the future, faults should develop due to
his non-compliance with the detailed requirements which we laid down.
I am afraid that the slight marks on the bath enamel cannot by any
stretch of the imagination come within this category, since there is
no evidence that they were caused by the carelessness of the workmen:
in saying this, I am not, as you put it "taking Grigblay's side" but
simply fulfilling my legal and professional obligation to see justice
done between the parties.

In the matter of the alleged "ley-line", I am at a loss to understand
your position. As I understand it, the only evidence for its existence
is the opinion of "Daddy" O'Gorman, the naturopath who collects and
dries herbs for Peregrine Hyphen-Hyphen. I can hardly believe that
Wanda's symptoms have anything to do with prehistoric ley-lines: this
is something upon which her GP could no doubt comment more knowledgeably.
We are certainly not prepared to contemplate any reduction of our fee
on these grounds.

I am sure that, in reflection, you will understand and agree with our
position.

Yours sincerely

JAMES

Parbuckle.   Barsetshire B.Sc.

Dear "Alf"   NEW HQ

     I gather that this is how you are addressed by your underlings. Let me make it quite plain that I am not one of them. But such is the decline in manners that no doubt we'll be Alf and Jim to one another before many suns have set.

     You tell me that your Directors have decreed that Tom, Dick & Harry are to be the M& E consultants for the HQ. This obviously demands a response, & I couldn't trust myself to give you a polite one off the cuff, by phone: hence this letter.

     I'm sorely tempted to describe them as "jumped-up plumbers (an expression actually used by a client) but that would hardly be fair. Technically, they are OK, but as collaborators with an architect they're disastrous. When it comes to working within a budget, one can only echo the words of the Duke of Wellington—"I don't know what effect they will have upon the subcontractors, but by God they terrify me."

     If your Directors insist, this is a cross we'll just have to bear. but if the options are still half-open we'd like to put up a couple of reliable alternatives, so that there can at least be some semblance of consultation — apart from anything else, the sooner your Board realises that our firm is not just a doormat the better for everyone concerned.

     Let's hear from you, Alfie-boy.

                 yours

               ~~Jim~~ J.L. Spinlove.

J Alphonse Parbuckle, ARICS, M.Inst.P.M., MISSP.
Property Manager
The Barsetshire Building Society
169 The High
BARCHESTER BX1 1MS

Dear Sir

Headquarters Building, Barchester
_____

Thank you for your letter of yesterday's date advising us that your
directors wish Messrs Thomson, Richards and Harriman to be appointed
as services consultants.

We cannot withhold approval from the appointment of this firm, with
whom we have worked in the past and whom we believe to be technically
competent in their own sphere. We would feel obliged, however, to
sound a note of caution.

Thomson Richards and Harriman's practice is accustomed to handling
projects in the engineering field in which the services of an architect
are not required or are, at most, marginal. In our experience, they do
not always readily accommodate themselves to working under the
co-ordination of an architect, or to a situation in which the costs of
the electrical, mechanical and heating installations have to be contained
within an overall budget for the building as a whole.

If your Board are not willing to accept alternative nominations, then we
shall work with Thomson Richards and Harriman to the best of our ability.
If, on the other hand, your directors are prepared to consider a choice
between, say, three reputable firms – including, needless to say,
Thomson Richards and Harriman – we are willing to suggest suitable
candidates and would wish to be present at any interview which they
may think proper to arrange.

Yours faithfully

SPINLOVE & SPINLOVE

Parbuckle. — Barsetshire B.Soc.

Dear Fatso,

New HQ

So you "desire acknowledgment of receipt" of your schedule of Requirements: do you, mon petit fonctionnaire? Your desire shall be gratified. I hereby acknowledge receipt.

Let me add that, at this stage, we are dealing with the basics — like spaces & circulation — & it doesn't help these thought-processes to confuse them with details such as bullet-proof glazing, which won't come into the picture for ages yet.

About that glazing — I bet you haven't read the B.S. I have (as of yesterday) & would point out that the grades of glass are defined by reference to six different kinds of weapon, from a 9 mm. Parabellum to a 12-bore. Perhaps you would care to tell us which mode of mayhem you anticipate. And don't say "Anticipate the worst", because I can't find any way of deciphering from the B.S. just which of these guns is the most dangerous. In the meantime, we'll do the obvious thing, i.e. we'll ask Pilkingtons for the most bullet-resistant glass on the market.

Get your trotters back in the trough, Fatso, and don't bother us again unless you absolutely have to.

Au revoir,
T.S

J Alphonse Parbuckle, ARICS, M.Inst.P.M., MISSP.
Property Manager
The Barsetshire Building Society
169 The High
BARCHESTER BX1 1MS

Dear Sir

New Headquarters

As requested, we are writing to confirm receipt of your Schedule of
Requirements. Once we have perused these, we shall be in touch in
order to discuss any items which may be in doubt.

In this connection, we note that you wish the cashiers' counter to
be protected by bullet-resistant glazing "to British Standard 5051:
Part I". We have studied this BS and there do seem to be certain
problems in applying it.

It provides for bullet-resistant glass to be classified under six
categories, ranging from attack by a 9mm Parabellum hand-gun to
attack by a 12 bore shot-gun. Obviously you would wish your staff
to be protected by the safest of these categories, but it is by no
means clear from the document which classification is the most
stringent, nor indeed why there should be any differentation at all,
considering that the nature of the weaponry which may be employed
is wholly unpredictable. Unless you have any specific requirements
in the matter, we shall consult with leading glass manufacturers
and come back to you.

We expect to be able to meet you on this and on any other queries
within the next few days.

Yours faithfully

SPINLOVE & SPINLOVE

Cal McGurk

Dear Mr. McG.   _Chateau McGurk_

What a surprise to find your confirmatory letter in the in-tray - from the sound of you on the 'phone last night. I'd expected that alcoholic amnesia would have obliterated your kind intentions, but I suppose all that Irn-Bru when you were a kid has given you a tough constitution.

Yes. I did see your picture in the "Leader," gripping the giant Pools cheque as if you were afraid it was going to take off & fly away, &, as you kindly suggest, I'll be glad to help you spend it. But take heed — you don't get much of a castle for £750,000 these days., even on your native heath.

Ignorant though I am as to the appropriate style for a mansion in Glen Drumlie, I'm even more ignorant of the laws, customs & techniques current in Pictland, & I don't propose to fall foul of them. So I suggest that our firm does the designing & we find a bunch of local trusties to guide us through the practicalities and legalities etc. That way, you won't have to pay us for travelling from the bottom to the top end of the U.K. every few days. And, before you mention it, let me say you _won't_ be "paying twice for the same job". the fee will be apportioned.

I'll make enquiries towards finding a Caledonian minder for us — they have an architectural institute up there which has a royal charter, so they can't all be painted blue, & I expect it can find someone. And I'll apply myself to the study of brochs, keeps, crannogs & fortresses, & be in touch shortly.

Keep your sporran padlocked & ignore the begging letters — you're going to need the entire jackpot for your chateau.   Yours

James

Mr Caliban McGurk
"Bide-a-Wee"
Chantry Avenue
BARCHESTER   BX1 3LM

Dear Mr McGurk

Proposed House at Drumliedubs

Thank you for your letter of the 23rd, confirming that you would
like us to design a mansion-house in Scotland for you. We are
glad to accept the commission which will be an intersting challenge.

We would advise splitting the architectural commission between the
design stage - which is obviously better handled here where we can
work in close touch with yourself - and the construction stage. It
would be very expensive for you to have us inspect work in progress
so far away and there are also differences in contracting and
construction practice to be considered. We would suggest that we
find a reliable firm of architects in Scotland to whom this part
of the work can be entrusted, the fee for the architectural services
being split accordingly.

We shall take advice on this and discuss it with you shortly, when
we shall also be taking instructions as to your requirements regarding
accommodation etc.

Yours sincerely

SPINLOVE & SPINLOVE

NOTES

Generally

The reader may notice that Spinlove upholds the tradition of giving his male clients the honorary rank of "esquire", despite the modern tendency to use "Mr". Quaint though it may seem, it has its points, especially when the addressee has a string of letters after his name and likes the look of them. "Joseph Soap, Esq. CBE" seems somehow to have a kind of dignity not conveyed by "Mr Jos. Soap CBE" which carries a faint suggestion that Jos. has Got Above His Station, possibly by methods which won't bear examination. But perhaps my views have been too much coloured by the office practice of my youth, when clients were assumed to be gentlemen and to expect "esquire", while contractors and clerks of works rated as tradesmen and got "Mr". Incidentally the most perfect example of social stratification in my experience was a factory plan, which showed a "Ladies' Toilet" for the office staff and a "Women's Lavatory" for the mill girls: but that was in 1914.

Spinlove often has to make up his mind whether he is "I" or "We". This has nothing to do with either schizophrenia or pretensions to royalty. It simply flows from the fact that "Spinlove & Spinlove" plainly denotes two people, and that one of them is dead. Actually, this gives him room for manoeuvre of a kind not available to his father, the original sole partner – that is, the convenience of adjusting the distance between himself and the other party and, on occasion, of depersonalising a situation which could cause discomfort if the protagonists were accustomed to using the more personal "I" form. The reader will find some interesting examples of Spinlove's use of this device, notably in letters, I, III, IV and VIII.

Letter I: Cast Not The First Stone

This is a tricky one. Quite apart from the libel aspect (although poor old Champagne Charlie is hardly likely to raise an action) a referee has to be fair both to the applicant and to the prospective employer. Indeed he could be in serious trouble if, in his reply, he suppressed a material fact: if Charlie were at that moment sleeping off a liquid lunch in Spinlove & Spinlove's outer office, James would have to be pretty careful not to let his good nature get in the way of his duty.

Not that he shows all that much good nature in his first draft. Indeed his feelings about poor old Malagrowther – plainly a man once respected but now well past his prime – are quite savage. One feels that at some point in their relationship Spinlove must have had a bad fright – the sort of fright a rock-climber might get from finding himself roped to a cripple.

To give him his due, he then brings his natural sense of fairness (as the architect son of an architect father, he has been raised in the belief that he should aim to be respected for fair dealing, whatever else) to bear on Malagrowther's present position, about which he knows next to nothing. A lot of things can change in eight years, for better as much as for worse – one of my own village's most notorious drunks ended her life as the teetotal housekeeper to a Salvation Army major. He is certainly bound to say what he obviously believes – that however "infirm of purpose" he may have been in the latter days of his connection with Spinlove & Spinlove, this man was, by training and early experience, superbly equipped for the work which he had to do – "One of the old school" as tradesmen say, half in praise and half in fear.

All in all, Spinlove extricates himself from this predicament as decently as one can. Such messages are necessarily coded. For instance, the reference to "traditional construction" and to the absence of "an unusually high content of electrical/mechanical services" are signals that Spinlove is not expressly recommending the man for work of a non-traditional and highly-serviced nature to which – even in his prime – his particular background might not be wholly relevant. The same goes for the reference to his non-membership of the Institute of Clerk of Works. "His health could have been better" is as far as Spinlove could decently go without actually leaning over backwards to cover up Malagrowther's physical problems. The most potentially damaging comment is one which it must have hurt Spinlove to set down in black and white – "He did however rely quite substantially on the presence and backing of the Architect". A good deal of the routine periodical inspection of building works is entrusted to quite junior architects and is, in fact, part of the process now dubbed "Continuing Professional Development". To them, the presence of an experienced and able Clerk of Works is invaluable, not only as an ever-present help in time of trouble, but as a source of information on all sorts of matters which the academic preparation for their careers seldom brings to light. In this respect, the Clerk of Works stands to the young architect as the staff nurse stands to the young hospital doctor. To suggest that Malagrowther might lean on that young man instead of supporting him is to warn the senior architect that he will have to take more of the duties of inspection on his own shoulders, and leave fewer of them to a junior. This could be bad news, but Spinlove has no alternative but to lay it on the line.

It is worth noting that, whereas he personally has been named as Malagrowther's referee, his final version is written entirely in the first person plural, as from Spinlove & Spinlove. In code, this could be a hint that he is distancing himself from the whole issue. Strictly speaking, he is making it clear that Malagrowther's relationship with him was wholly professional – that is, a relationship with Spinlove & Spinlove – and not the sort of relationship which would call for a wholly personal character-reference, as for example, one from his parish priest, rabbi, imam or G.P.

Letter II: Retort Courteous

This letter raises some interesting points.

The Director's reminder must have been tactless enough to touch Spinlove on a raw nerve, but the reply is a notable over-reaction.

"Sir", *by itself*, was a rather formal style of salutation even a hundred years ago, when the writer signed-off with "I remain, Sir, your obedient servant". Today it would be considered distinctly peremptory, almost like a challenge to a duel: certainly much too brusque for Spinlove's present purpose.

If you want to put on paper that your correspondent is an "impudent liar", make sure that you put it in writing and give it to him in a sealed envelope with your own hand. Otherwise your typist and his secretary will both read it (and not necessarily keep it to themselves) and thus you could be held to have "published" that opinion. Libel actions are expensive enough to be fairly uncommon, but Spinlove's draft amounts to a declaration of war, and who knows how the addressee might have reacted.

You will note that Spinlove had prudently kept the cleared cheques which his bank returns with each monthly statement. Apart from being invaluable in clearing up misunderstandings like this one, it is the kind of careful business practice which keeps his accountant happy.

It is perhaps surprising that the Chamber of Commerce had not already asked for payment by direct debit, as do many bodies who levy an annual subscription. Maybe Spinlove disliked his current account being debited with an amount for which he had not consciously signed a cheque: I must admit to feeling that way myself.

Letter III: Red Alert

There is a saying "Never make a client of a friend: always make a friend of a client". Neither option should be swallowed whole.

An architect who is commissioned to design a one-off private house (not as common an experience today as it used to be) inevitably becomes drawn into a greater familiarity with the client than if he were designing for a committee, if only because personal preferences in the most intimate areas of domestic bliss may be shyly disclosed to him. This makes it very difficult when, as may well happen at the final reckoning, he has to present himself in the role of stern arbitrator between two parties to a sternly commercial contract. In that latter capacity, he has to resist tears and blandishments on the one side and hard-luck stories on the other. And while long experience has taught the building contractor that he can expect justice from Mr Spinlove, but nothing more, the Thynngses have had no such initiation. Presumably, Quintin has set Wanda Rose on to soften-up nice Jimmy Spinlove, a task to which she is not averse, and for which she seems to have been preparing the ground.

In the circumstances, his first draft is not all that bad, but the final version is much better.

It will be noted that the lady is "Mrs Wanda Rose Thynnges" in Spinlove's draft, but "Mrs Q. St. J. Thynnges" in the letter as sent. Probably his secretary made the change off her own bat, knowing that the former style is strictly correct until Wanda became a widow or divorcee; this delicate distinction is generally ignored in present-day office practice but it, in this case, does help to put a little more distance between Wanda and Jimmy, and it looks as if he could do with it.

Letter IV: Action Stations

Spinlove and Cypher are old friends and often lunch together. Hence the informality of the draft, and the outspoken way in which Spinlove refers to his colleague's shortcomings. Bills of Quantities are, in theory, a full and accurate itemised quantification of the work and materials comprised in the sum for which the contractor undertakes the job, and, when priced item by item, will produce a figure which (apart from variations specifically ordered or approved by the architect) will be the final cost to the client of the whole operation. This is, of course, a platonic ideal, requiring superhuman foresight and accuracy on the part of everyone involved in the pre-tendering process. Consequently, surveyors tend to err on the safe side, even where the tender is to allow a provisional sum for "contingencies": and wise surveyors tend to conceal their true margin for error until the last possible moment, suspecting (not always wrongly) that the architect will blow it all prematurely. This seems to be what this architect and his clients have in fact managed to do, because Spinlove assumed, from long dealings with Cypher and Cypher, that they had kept more up their sleeve than was actually the case.

Spinlove's letter, as sent, is conspicuously more formal than the draft: he is "we" from start to finish, for instance. This is not a mark of his displeasure but a proper precaution. If the worst comes to the worst and the writs start flying, the correspondence between architect and quantity surveyor may well have to be produced in court or in an arbitration, and their transactions will appear to have been more carefully and responsibly conducted in terms of "Dear Sirs" than of "Jimmy" and "Joe".

Letter V: Anything to Declare

The first draft is definitely no way to set about renewing your insurance, unless you are prepared for a swingeing increase in premium. But, as we know, Spinlove had already been warned about his outspokenness, and was quite submissive when it came to signing the final version, although he could hardly resist a little dig in his answer to Question 7. He was only human, and like most of us, had an ambivalent attitude to his insurers. From one point of view, they are guardian angels ready to step in when disaster strikes: from another, they are impudent inquisitors, requiring information which, if falsely or carelessly given, can disqualify the insured from obtaining any benefit whatsoever. The blunt facts are that they are quoting a price for covering a risk: that they will base the price on a guesstimate of the risk: that they will base the guesstimate on parameters which they think relevant and that they expect full and truthful answers to the questions which they imagine (rightly or wrongly) will establish certain probabilities. You either want the insurance cover or you do not: if you do, then you have to do your best to make sense out of the questions, however silly they may look.

Hence Spinlove's eventual careful answer to Question 10, which asked him whether he *ensured* that such specialists as structural or services engineers entered into binding contracts with the client for the proper performance of their duties.

Hence also his answer to Question 12, which asked for particulars of any considerations which might affect the risk and had not been brought out elsewhere in the questionnaire. It is unlikely that Grigblays would put up a defective house and if they did, the blame could hardly be laid at Spinlove's door, given the limited service which he undertook to provide. Nevertheless, nobody is infallible and an aggrieved house-purchaser raising an action against Grigblay might be advised to join Spinlove in the action ("he's insured, old boy – no skin off his nose") thus involving him in lawyers' fees, if nothing worse. In that event, his insurers would definitely not be amused to hear that the products of his lively creative imagination included, say, eighty identical houses, each with potentially the same defect, none of which appears in his return of "value of work certified". That value is, after all, one of the insurers' main parameters for the extent of their risk.

It was thoughtful of Spinlove to mention that Grigblay and Son are registered with the National House-Building Council. If the insurers know anything at all about the building industry (which Spinlove clearly and not unjustifiably doubts, judging from their questionnaire) they will recognise that he is not putting his head on the block for a bunch of cowboys.

Letter VI: Pay Up or Else

On the face of it, Spinlove's familiarity with the poetry of Robert Burns is remarkable, but probably he went straight from the newspaper report to the Oxford Dictionary of Quotations, looking for ammunition. Not the best way to go about collecting what must have been quite a small fee. If he had dug a little deeper into Burns, he would have come upon the lines:

> *Know prudent, cautious self-control*
> *is wisdom's root.*

The reference to dirks, claymores and sporrans are tasteless, to say the least, even allowing for Spinlove's habit of overkill. On the other hand, he probably felt that McGurk was asking for it by being photographed in the Garb of Old Gaul in darkest Barsetshire, spouting verses by a shamelessly honest poet while back at the Motor Mecca he is reneging on a trifling debt.

Having got this off his chest in draft, Spinlove shows a proper grasp of the realities of life in the Age of Credit. One of the benefits (or problems, depending on your cash-flow position) of carrying on business in a small town is that no businessman wants heads to be discreetly shaken when his name comes up over the G-and-Ts: still less does he want his credit rating to diminish in the eyes of any of the agencies who might be asked to vouch for it. Spinlove's reference to "cash flow problems" is a gentle hint.

It will fall on deaf ears, of course, if most of the Motor Mecca's deals are put through on the basis of wads of used notes. In that case, the "heavies" may be the only people who could recover Spinlove's fee, provided he could overcome his bourgeois distaste for employing agents whose knuckles brush the ground. But he ought not to commit this thought to paper, for any suggestion of "harassment" could go against him in a courtroom.

Much better is his delicate allusion to "my agents", a term which can mean anything from Razor Eddie to Spinlove's family lawyers, Messrs. Peabody, Doolittle and Leake. In between, there are debt-collecting agencies old and new who are paid by subscription and commission, and Spinlove may well be a subscriber to one of them. Meantime, he is keeping his cards as close to his chest as his volatile temperament permits.

Significantly, he departs here from his normal practice of making his client an "esquire". Mister McGurk has clearly fallen from grace. And Spinlove & Spinlove are definitely "we" all the way through.

Letter VII: No Thank You

Spinlove must surely have preserved the memory of his family's disastrous experience with the original "Riddoppo" back in 1926 – probably it had become a family legend. Otherwise he would hardly have taken such a sledgehammer to what was presumably a harmless, if smarmy, invitation of a kind which architects receive with monotonous frequency.

The eventual reply is, of course, pure hypocrisy. He would have been quite able to attend the ghastly lunch and boring demonstration if he had wanted to, and plainly could have had no regrets about not doing so. However this is a harmless and normal formula for painlessly rejecting an invitation. Riddoppo Ltd. would perhaps have done better to send him a returnable card with the usual "I shall/shall not ..." formula printed on it, rather than the sort of deckle-edged letter which he described as an "effusion".

Letter VIII: Just One of Those Knights

It has to be said for Spinlove that he is not by nature afflicted by a need to cringe before people of title or wealth, even in the way of business. He was brought up in the belief that the profession of architecture confers a kind of inherent dignity on people who practise it honestly and meet its manifold problems without panicking or prevaricating. This said, his first reaction to Sir Midas's civil and concerned enquiry does him no credit.

To be fair, one of the more tiresome tasks which an architect has to face is explaining an essentially aesthetic decision to a client who does not accept, as a basic article of faith, that the architect is endowed with perfect taste in the way that some musicians are gifted with perfect pitch. "He that filches from me my good name" as Shakespeare remarked "robs me of that which not enriches him and makes me poor indeed". Substitute "aesthetic judgement" for "good name" and you have the attitude – not an unreasonable one – of the architect who, in his heart of hearts, knows that this is the one faculty which, acquired by intensive training, distinguishes him from the many different kinds of technical experts who would like to take over his function.

Any argument with the client – aesthetic argument most of all – is not easy when the client is accustomed to being obeyed simply because he is rich: it is made even more difficult when he is not really the client, in the legal sense at all, but merely the most influential and vocal member of a committee: and more difficult still when this "client" is expressing his doubts for the best of all possible motives – the desire to produce a worthy building.

This motive is too often obscured from the architect by the fact that his supposed adversary does not normally share with him a common language in which matters of "taste" can be soberly discussed. It would not be difficult to convince Sir Midas that he is having the wool pulled over his eyes by Spinlove's mastery of architectural jargon, and Spinlove has obviously convinced himself that he is stuck with the task of explaining quite a recondite point of aesthetics to an old fool whose eyes have been blinded by gazing at the movements of the money market on his V.D.U. and who understands no language but that of the balance sheet.

So it is all the more credit to him that he does eventually work round to the realisation that he and the old buffer are really on the same side, and goes on from there to make a serious and honest effort at rationalising a choice which was originally essentially an intuitive one: after all, it has been said that "intuition is instant logic". The exercise was almost certainly good for Spinlove himself: once he overcame his irritation it may even have given him a good deal of pleasure, of the kind that a mathematician or philosopher gets from an "elegant" proof.

His final form of words makes it quite clear that he knows what he is talking about and this is what matters. It may not be possible to explain his decision – which, after all, is founded on the experience of years of experimentation – in terms simple enough to be understood by someone whose own experiments have been in a wholly different field. But Sir Midas made his fortune by hiring people who know their job and he recognises their inimitable style when he hears it: especially when it is expressed with the courtesy which he expects of a relatively young and not very rich professional man in an obscure provincial town. Probably Spinlove will have no further trouble in this direction. With luck, he will get a letter of thanks for his patient and lucid explanation – maybe even a pat on the back at the next meeting of the Building Committee.

Letter IX: The Sting

Oh dear! Peregrine is presumably related to Sir Midas; he may even have mentioned Spinlove's name, in the honeymoon period five years earlier, as a thoroughly able and conscientious chap, and very reasonable moneywise. But that was a long time ago, and perhaps the antiques and bygones business has not been prospering: it could be that Peregrine lacks the Midas touch. Besides, somebody has told him that all these architect fellers are insured up to the hilt, so it's no skin off old Spinlove's nose: "Won't cost him a penny and you could get a new roof out of it".

Only half true. Spinlove's professional indemnity insurance policy will have an "excess" clause by which he has to bear the first (say) £1000 of each and every claim, besides which his future premiums will obviously go up if he comes out as a bad risk. So he has every inducement to repudiate this claim, even if he did not regard it – as he obviously does – as a gratuitous and unwarranted slur on his firm's reputation.

In the end, he pursues the wise course of saying no more than he has to. His insurers would have been happy to have him simply say "We deny any liability" and no more, but Spinlove's aim is to head off his antagonist from any precipitate lawsuit – not good publicity, money apart – by making it plain that he knows where the blame really lies. Hard luck, Peregrine – almost everybody in the business of lifting heavy loads imagines that this is what roofs are for, whether they were designed that way or not. But he shouldn't have tried to sting honest James Spinlove. As the notice in the French zoo is supposed to have said "This animal is vicious – if attacked, it will defend itself".

Letter X: Toeing The Line

This follows naturally from the complaint by Peregrine Hyphen-Hyphen. Professional indemnity insurers normally make it a "condition precedent" to meeting claims against the insured that such claims are notified as soon as they arise. It is something which obviously sticks in Spinlove's throat. Apart from the libel problems which were mentioned earlier – and which reflected on his temperament, rather than his professional ability – Spinlove probably had a blameless, or at least claimless, record in the eyes of his insurers. He is probably right in saying that this one will be pursued no further. Nevertheless, he has to toe the line. He will be asked about it each time he renews his insurance, and on each occasion he will be a little bit apprehensive about the effect on his premium. Damn Peregrine Hyphen-Hyphen and his blasted junk-shop......

Letter XI: Fools Rush In

One of the stimulating things about a modest provincial practice is that you meet all kinds. One day, Spinlove is sipping a daiquiri with *arriviste* Quintin and sultry Wanda: on another he finds himself trading insights with Sir Midas across the highly-polished boardroom table at St Walpurgis': anon he is persuading the planners to let Caliban McGurk convert the old slaughter-house into a boneyard for clapped-out automobiles. All grist to the mill, as they say. And now he has to take on the job of educating mine genial host Bill Sikes in the matter of chimneys and where to put them.

Publicans are well known to be problem clients. So are clergymen, doctors and academics, but for different reasons. Publicans do not normally claim concessions in the matter of fees on the grounds that such concessions are sanctioned by traditional respect for the selflessness of their vocation or on the grounds that their education qualifies them to argue the hind leg off any donkey who disagrees with them. The sin of the publican is simply the other side of the talent by which he keeps a comfortable and sociable bar: he is all things to all men. Sikes would have been a saint if he had kept the chimney-sweep's opinion to himself. Not being a saint, he saw no harm in scribbling it on the back of a menu and shoving it in the post.

How was he to know that it would hit one of his architect's tender spots? Next to being contradicted on aesthetic matters, Spinlove was clearly acutely sensitive about any slur on his practical capacities. He was probably well aware that his client would encourage opinions from every bricklayer, plasterer, carpenter and plumber in the bar about every step in the building operation, and that he would just have to roll with the punch. But a chimneysweep ....

His sneer at the sweep in the tail-end of his draft is really quite unpardonable, positively Victorian in its *de haut en bas* attitude to a perfectly respectable, hardworking (and probably quite well-off) tradesman who has every bit as much right to be in the lounge bar as Spinlove has. But there is no reason to suppose that this is mere snobbery, since Spinlove curls his lip just as much when it is a knight who calls his opinion in question. Some people would call it professional arrogance, but really it is quite the opposite – a sense of insecurity bred of the knowledge that nobody can hope to be infallible across the whole spectrum of the know-how which the modern architect is expected to possess. He will be feeling much more relaxed when he meets Mr Sikes at the Old Crocks Get-together.

Incidentally, it was convenient that his (or his father's) system of plan storage and filing enabled him to locate that girder. For all the inconvenience of keeping them, these old plans can be an asset to a practice in a small town in which buildings are altered more than once in their lifetime.

Letter XII: We Can All Make Them

We can indeed, but this one will give Joe Cypher a particularly red face. The quantity surveyor's essential and fundamental skill, from which his job gets its name, is the preparation of bills of quantities. These are expected to provide the builder with an accurate, itemised and quantified breakdown of the work described in the architect's drawings, which, when priced-out item by item, will enable him to calculate a sensible lump sum to offer as his price for the job. Although these Bills are expected to give a complete and accurate account of the work, they are not warranted as such: quantity surveyors and architects are no less fallible than other humans. Consequently, all normal building contracts provide for the contract sum to be varied (either upwards or downwards) not only by changes of intention on the part of the architect – formally recorded as Architect's Instructions – but by the rectification of omissions in the bills due to human error. Assuming that the omitted work is shown on the architect's contract drawings, the rectification of the surveyor's error requires no further action, and Gradgrind knows this perfectly well. But he also knows that he is expected, at the end of the job, to produce an itemised statement showing how the final sum due to the contractor is arrived at, and he would prefer each variation to be identified by reference to an Architect's Instruction (often loosely called a "Variation Order") rather than as an error on his own part.

In this case, Cypher & Cypher have dropped a real clanger by omitting the whole of the roof-tiling over the stables. Admittedly not every new house these days has stables attached to it (Wanda and Quintin are perhaps exceptionally upwardly-mobile) but that is no excuse – the work has been plainly shown on Spinlove's drawings. So Spinlove is quite correct in saying that the correction in money terms requires no action by him.

He is also correct in suspecting that, by issuing a retrospective "instruction" for work which is already amply described in his contract drawings, he could be walking into a minefield. Even the most honest building firm has a duty to its shareholders to collect every penny which can be extracted from diligent reading of the small print. Spinlove's sensitive ears detect the faint rumble of breakers ahead and, as we shall soon see, he is not mistaken.

Jim and Joe are old friends, hence the former's barely concealed envy of the imagined life-style of the latter: it is common for architects to believe quite sincerely (and not always wrongly) that they are existing on the smell of an oily rag compared with their counterparts in the money-managing professions who are living the life of Riley. Spinlove is probably being quite unfair. Joe Cypher is more likely to be vacationing at Marbella than at Moustique. And serve him right.

Letter XIII: In The Eye Of The Beholder

Spinlove's dislike of ill-formed criticism has already been remarked upon: here it is close to boiling point. Given the nearly impossible task of grafting something decent on to the vulgar carcase of St Walpurgis, he would probably have had a difficult time with the client committee – one of whom, as we know, concerns himself with the most intimate details and carries no mean clout – and now he is in for a replay at the hands of the bureaucracy. He is doubly enraged by the fact that this particular arm of the bureaucracy, charged though it may be with the cause of the community's architectural values, is not staffed, as it might have been forty years earlier, by architect-planners but by experts in land-use whose basic education and approach to architectural matters differs significantly from his own. Hence the savagery of his proposed attack on poor Mr Trollope whose telephone call was probably no more than an attempt to find out whether Spinlove could come up with a ready-made answer to questions which his committee might well feel bound to ask.

The architect's one good card is the near-certainty that Sir Midas, once convinced of the merit of the design, is not going to change his mind and, if called upon, will only be too glad to put his mouth where his money is. In the final version, Spinlove plays this card with some skill: in the first draft he slammed it on the table rather too violently. In both cases, he realised that aesthetic opinions are always subjective and difficult to argue before a committee, whereas the sort of punch packed by Sir Midas and his potential allies is something else again.

It was sensible to suggest a meeting: Spinlove had no doubt become fluent by this time in the oral presentation of his case and in the unlikely event of his being over-ruled he will at least have justified himself in Sir Midas's eyes as "a bonny fighter".

As we shall see however, there are still breakers ahead: before he is finished, the words "St Walpurgis" may well be graven on his heart.

Letter XIV: Umpire!

There is something touching about Spinlove's response to this request. He is, after all, a mature architect respected in his community, with a reputation for fair dealing. Yet he is obviously flattered by this invitation to settle a dispute which is almost certainly technical, and comfortably within his expertise.

Well, so he should be. An arbitrator is not merely a mutual friend – although the term "amicable" may appear in his terms of reference – but, once he accepts office, is a lay judge endowed with very substantial powers which he may not lightly abuse. It is wise of Spinlove – no doubt he has been consulting his own solicitor – to wish the exact terms of his appointment to be submitted to him before he accepts office. Apart from anything else, he must be sure that the parties are not, wittingly or unwittingly, tying his hands behind his back by depriving him of any of the powers which otherwise would, under common law, implicitly be his: more importantly, his award could be challenged if he were either to go beyond the limits of the dispute submitted to him or to fail to deal with all the questions submitted. So he must start off with a document which states, with some precision, what is expected of him.

Spinlove is also well aware of the possibility that the parties may only need "their heads banged together" as he elegantly puts it. Many arbitrations, often about ridiculously small amounts of money, are no more than a transposition into business terms of the urge which makes a pair of stags wrestle interminably antler-to-antler on a hillside. Neither wants to be called "chicken" and all that is really required is a verdict by a mutually-respected third party, so that loss of money is not equated with loss of face.

It is a sad feature of our increasingly litigious society (a feature for which its natural beneficiaries, the lawyers, are not blameless) that this process may end up with not only solicitors but counsel appearing for both sides and bringing with them the assumption on which trial by jury – that cornerstone of so much court procedure – is based; namely that every issue has to be spelt out and argued orally in terms which will extract a just verdict out of people who are neither technically nor legally expert, guided by a judge who will be well-versed in jurisprudence but may be wholly ignorant of the technicalities of building. In cases where a man of skill and honour can get to the root of the matter merely by studying the admitted exchanges between the parties – and especially where the parties have boxed themselves into a corner from which they simply want such a man to extricate them with minimum hassle and loss of face – there is much to be said for simplifying the process.

Spinlove is probably right in guessing that this is such a case and it is interesting that he seems to have invented off the top of his head a device very similar to the "Note of Proposed Findings" which, in arbitrations under

Scots law, is the normal prelude to the publication of the final Award. It has the considerable advantage of cutting the feet from a party who might wish to challenge the final award on the grounds that the arbitrator has failed to deal with all the points submitted or, alternatively, has gone beyond the issues submitted. It also has the practical advantage of allowing the parties the satisfaction of having their respective arguments scrupulously examined even if they have not had a formal hearing.

If the parties intimate acceptance of his proposed ruling, he will ratify it in the shape of a formal Award, on whose wording one hopes he will consult a friendly lawyer. If they demur – well, at least he gave them the chance to cut their losses, and he can appoint his own personal "minder" (properly called his "Clerk and Legal Adviser") secure in the knowledge that this functionary's fees – like his own – will form part of the costs of the arbitration and are, to all intents and purposes, not subject to argument or negotiation.

It should be noted that Spinlove has apparently been invited under a contractual agreement which provides for arbitration by someone mutually agreed by the parties – in other words, someone whom both sides trust to deal fairly – rather than by a nominee of some professional or trade organisation who may well be, as Spinlove suspects, a very expensive metropolitan mandarin. The businessmen of Barchester are to be congratulated on upholding the ancient provincial habit of keeping their family rows within the family.

Are we to believe that Mr Stryver really employs juniors who get tired and emotional during the lunch-hour (they should be so lucky) or is Spinlove perhaps confusing his Mr Carton with an earlier Mr Stryver's assistant?

Letter XV: Don't Shoot The Pianist

This letter is something of a joker in the pack. Instead of an abrasive draft followed by a mellower final version, we have here a meek draft replaced by a much more resolute rewrite. There must be a reason.

The reason must surely be in the developing relationship between Spinlove and Sir Midas.

No architect should be tempted to dash into print to defend his work unless his back is really to the wall: the apposite proverb is *"Qui s'excuse, s'accuse"*. But Spinlove must have been truly horrified when the Friends of Barsetshire pulled the plug on a design for which his best-heeled patron would be signing the cheque: hence his immediate urge to justify himself.

In his first reaction, however, he did less than justice to the temperament of Sir Midas. The hyphenated knight did not make his fortune by backing losers or hiring no-hopers, and he would not wish to be advertised by the Friends of Barsetshire, or anyone else, as the sort of man who would do so. I think it is reasonable to suppose that Spinlove, before dashing into print, would, as an act of courtesy, have made discreet enquiries as to the propriety of doing so: he may have indicated the line which he proposed to take. It would be entirely in character for Sir Midas to have responded "Far too mild – never complain, never explain, never apologise – take the gloves off and give 'em hell".

Neither letter, of course, could placate the Friends of Barsetshire since the criteria employed by their more vocal members have plainly been skewed by the hundred-year-old tendency to judge buildings as *objets d'art et de vertu* instead of as places and components of place. The antiquarian faction have, on their side, the authority of the proverb "Better not mix the breeds": on those terms, the continuation of the Venetian style, whatever its faults, would be preferable to the introduction of a compromise which would have, like Power's mule, "neither pride of ancestry nor hope of posterity". Spinlove probably had rather more respect for this view than for the other – presumably rather trendier – faction of the Friends which would put about the rather faded cliché that "a good uncompromisingly modern building will always sit happily alongside a good old building". In the absence of any generally-accepted definition of "the good", this simplistic axiom has served to justify, in all our cities, the jostling of treasured buildings by brash intruders whose claim to be "good" rests upon the plausibility of their advocates before the planning committee rather than upon anything approaching a consensus on absolute values.

The sad thing is that, in the last analysis, it is the Friends and their like who are so often the last line of defence against those who would, wittingly or unwittingly, destroy a community's attachment to its own place and that they are, like the Poor Bloody Infantry so often in history, desperately ill-equipped for the task. This is a problem far too large to be explored here, and Spinlove obviously recognises, as he writes, that he is teetering on the brink of a horribly wide void in human understanding. Let us give him credit for having extricated himself with a certain amount of dignity. No doubt the secretary of the Friends – faced, like all his kind, with the need to fill-up next year's syllabus – responded with an invitation to give them a little chat.

Letter XVI: Good Try, But ......

As Spinlove sensed earlier, Grigblay's in-house surveyor has detected a whiff of an opportunity of claiming extra money and has pursued it with the terrier-like instinct of his breed.

A small text-book could be written around this particular confrontation but this is not the place for it: indeed, light-minded readers would be well advised to skip the rest of this Note.

Suffice it to say, that the terms under which building contracts are normally let – that is the conditions of what was originally the "RIBA Form of Contract", became the "Standard Form of Contract" and is now generally called the "JCT Form of Contract" – have always allowed the possibility that a contractor's operations may be held up through no fault of his own, and have therefore provided that the prescribed contract completion date should be extended. The grounds for such legitimate extension are laid down very carefully in the contract conditions.

Some of them – such as strikes – only entitle the contractor to a relaxation of the completion date, and hence to a remission of the sum of which he would be mulcted in damages for non-completion. One, in particular, entitles him to much, much more, and that is: dithering on the part of the architect. An architect who brings the work to a standstill because he cannot bring himself to tell the contractor, at the proper time, what he is supposed to do is plainly falling down on the job and this is recognised by imposing what amounts to a penalty on the building owner (he being a party to the contract, whereas the architect is not) which he can, hopefully, recover from his erring agent, the architect. The penalty takes the form of obliging the building owner to reimburse the contractor for "direct loss and expense" incurred through the architect's delay.

The mere fact that many legal brains of the first order have debated the interpretation of "direct" in this context indicates that it is a field into which nobody should willingly stray. If Spinlove were to issue a retrospective "Architect's Instruction" which could be interpreted as admitting a delay by him, Grigblay's surveyor would not hesitate to use it to justify a claim for such matters as three weeks' additional plant-hire, four weeks' extra use of site-huts and other ingenious items which, between them, would obliterate any claim against Grigblay for delay and probably leave him comfortably in pocket.

It is of course, a piece of effrontery to invoke in this context a contract condition aimed against work being brought to a standstill through indecision on the part of the architect or his client: Spinlove's intentions were completely and accurately described in drawings which were in the contractor's possession from the point at which he was invited to tender. Moreover, this condition can only be invoked with a substantial degree of formality – specifically in writing and not substantially remote in time from the point at which the contractor could reasonably expect to have the architect's decision. Grigblay seems to have ignored this formality and to be asking Spinlove, long after the event, to issue an instruction for work for which no further instructions – the stable tiling having already been clearly shown on the contract drawings – is required, and his (or his surveyor's) aim is clearly to catch Spinlove bending.

However, he has picked the wrong man. Spinlove's final letter demonstrates a proper awareness of his own position and of his clients' interests, and a proper concern for fair dealing between the two parties to the contract without the intemperate (albeit justified) language of the first draft. The reference to Grandpa Grigblay in that draft is a little below the belt. Spinlove, at his father's knee, had old man Grigblay held out to him as an exemplar of all that was best in the old-time builder. Young Grigblay, however, is merely a shareholder – and maybe a minority one – in a limited liability company which, as a witty American put it, is a species which "has neither a soul to be saved nor a backside to be kicked" and it is entirely possible that he has over him a Chairman who is more likely to have been raised as a Chartered Accountant than as a building craftsman. *O tempora, o mores.*

It is not very usual for an architect to remind the contractor that, if all else fails, he has the right to call for arbitration. Spinlove is warning Grigblay that, as far as he, Spinlove is concerned, all else *has* failed and this question is not negotiable: from now on, Grigblay had better be prepared to put his money where his mouth is.

Letter XVII: Noblesse Oblige

Spinlove was obviously drunk when he scribbled the draft on the back of a winelist at *La Rotisserie de la Reine Pedauque,* Barchester's most upmarket eaterie: analysis of the ring-marks would probably prove them to be from a very drinkable claret. He would not be the first architect to buy himself a good lunch on the strength of a plum job.

Sir Midas has come round, in Spinlove's view, from being a myopic dotard to being a worthy sparring-partner: not a bad basis for the development of a friendship. Anyway, he has plainly convinced Sir Midas that he is no push-over and, as already noticed, this is a powerful recommendation.

Spinlove's final letter errs, if anything, on the effusive side. It would have been more dignified without the paragraph beginning "On a purely personal note ......" which does rather suggest that the writer is lying on his back, wagging his tail and asking for his tummy to be tickled. But he knows his man better than we do – maybe Sir Midas likes it laid on with a trowel. It does, at least, sweeten the pill of the warning which Spinlove has deftly inserted in the preceding sentence.

Once the Royal Fine Art Commission is dragged in, on top of the Friends of Barsetshire and Mr Trollope of the Planning Department, Spinlove could be in for a rough ride. "A challenge which we welcome" is architect's code for "a cross which we will have to bear, and we hope that our tribulations will be reflected in the fee".

Her Ladyship here makes her first and only appearance: a sensitive ear can detect the tinkle of teacups in the background. It is possible that she is not immune to the mature charm which worked so powerfully on Wanda Rose Thynnges, and this may have helped to bring her husband into his present benevolent state of mind. But that is pure speculation.

Letter XVIII: Let's Face The Music And Dance

It looks as though the architect and quantity surveyor have been called to face the music in the matter of the omitted roofing. A bit hard on poor Spinlove, whose duty of co-ordinating the work of the ancillary professionals could hardly be supposed to extend to checking their arithmetic. A little rough, too, on Joe Cypher. Granted that a quantity surveying firm can be expected to devise its office routines so that the quantities are, at least, fully measured, it remains a fact that mistakes can be made, even in the best-regulated families, and probably would never have come to light if final adjustment of the contract sum had brought it out below the original tender instead of above it. In that event, even a nitpicker like Quintin Thynnges would probably never have interested himself in the details of Cypher and Cypher's Final Measurement and Valuation: whereas it is plain that he has and – since he is no fool in money matters – has discerned, among the thicket of figures and cross-references, this not unsubstantial extra.

Like many another who had detected feet of clay under the trouser-cuffs of his professional advisers, he is yielding to the urge to cut them (or at least, their fees) down to size and in his present mood he is not too particular how he sets about it. A mistake on his part, since Spinlove (as we have seen) has a strong sense of justice and a passionate attachment to his professional role as a dispenser of it: he finds sharp practice just as intolerable on a client's part as on a contractor's.

Money problems with the Thynngeses were, of course, always to be expected and it was wise of Spinlove to get them committed to writing rather than to explode over the telephone. Quintin may well be the sort of man who prefers not to pay a bill until he is handed a writ. In this case, he seems to be attacking on three fronts.

He would like the omitted tiling to be offset against Joe Cypher's fee, or even to have it knocked off Grigblay's final instalment. He would like something from somebody – either Grigblay or Spinlove – for the marks on the bath enamel. And he would like to find some way of cutting Spinlove's fee.

On the first of these, he is on to a non-starter. He enjoys the benefit of a roof built exactly as his architect designed it, and for no more money that it would have cost him had Cypher and Cypher got their sums right in the first place. If the rectification of the error had caused a substantial loss – like obliging the Thynngeses to sell valuable assets at the bottom of the market – he might have some claim for recompense. But if his father-in-law is (as Spinlove suspects) picking up the tabs, this would be a difficult claim to substantiate, even in the total over-run of £273 on the cost of a large private house were not, comparatively speaking, a trifle. Thynnges would have done better to follow the maxim "To err is human, to forgive divine" and be remembered as a decent, sensible chap.

On the second score, Spinlove's final draft makes quite a decent job of explaining the status of an architect's final certificate, a subject on which many thousands of words have been written and many wigs wagged in courts of law. His inspections must have been thorough indeed if, at the end of the day, the clients have found no more to complain about than these minute blemishes. Considering that the architect's normal scale fee covers only periodical and general inspections, not constant and detailed superintendence, the Thynngeses probably got far better value out of Spinlove than they are being asked to pay for. He knows it too, which is why he feels entitled to be very incensed at his client's attempt to get still more blood along with his pound of flesh by trying to cash in on "Daddy" O'Gorman's theories about ley-lines.

If "Daddy" is an associate of Peregrine Hyphen-Hyphen, who seems to be expanding his antiques and bygones business towards the darker shores of folklore, there might be just a suspicion of residual ill-feeling somewhere. But more likely he is just a homespun guru with a taste for science-fiction and a habit of running off at the mouth.

The last sentence of Spinlove's final letter is almost meaningless if read literally. It is, in fact, a coded message. It is business-speak for "Don't try to argue – I have a good lawyer".

Letter XIX: A Walk On Thin Ice

This is even thinner ice than the episode of Champagne Charlie Malagrowther.

The cost of a substantial building project will today be accounted for, in large part, by electrical, heating and mechanical works which, by their nature, require specialist attention – preferably by a consultant appointed by the client to work hand-in-hand with the architect. Common sense dictates that such specialist collaborators should be recruited by the architect himself, on the basis of their proven capacity to work hand-in-hand with him towards a common end – the satisfaction of the client's needs. Unfortunately, common sense is not always the controlling factor.

Idiosyncratic members of a commissioning body may be enthusiastic for a particular firm of consultants, just as Sir Midas was for Spinlove himself. Indeed, Harriman could have had a friend who was quite prepared to lay it on the line that Thomson Richards and Harriman's appointment as consultants was his trade-off for Spinlove's appointment as architect – a deal which would not upset Sir Midas one whit, and would not be disclosed to Spinlove. If so, the ice is exceptionally thin. Equally (and more particularly in the public sector where the Government Auditor's nose is ever keen to detect a whiff of corruption) the idea of distancing the specialists from the architect, even to the point of assembling total strangers into a so-called "team", has undeniable attractions from the point of view of the upright bureaucrat, whatever mayhem it may inflict on the design process. The architect can, of course, claim the right to reject a "collaborator" with whom he cannot hope to collaborate successfully. But this is not a right which one can invoke lightly and normally will not risk invoking at all, unless the client's nominee is not only unacceptable but demonstrably incapable or dishonest. In the normal way, no properly-accredited consulting engineer is likely to fall into either of these categories: which makes it all the more difficult for the architect to register a disapproval based on more subjective and subtle reasons, however pessimistic he may be about developing a fruitful working relationship with someone who is more accustomed to working as an independent expert than as a team-member – as appears to be the case with Thomson Richards and Harriman.

Spinlove is wise to sound a note of caution, in view of the method by which the subcontractors for such works as electrical, heating, ventilating and mechanical works are commonly appointed. Whereas the architect is expected to design the building works in considerable – even, some would say, in immaculate – detail, the engineer is not usually required to live up to any such unrealistic expectation. He assumes that each of the firms who will eventually be invited to tender for the engineering sub-contracts will have its own expertise and its own method of meeting his overall requirements, and will price according to that method: in the first instance, the consultant will simply recommend a provisional sum which, in his opinion, will cover any specialist tenders likely to be obtained.

Practically, this old-established custom has much to be said for it: engineers have not yet been coerced into the position (so carelessly accepted by the architectural profession) of posing as experts in teaching their grandmothers how to suck eggs. Administratively, however, it can play hell with the architect's efforts to produce an acceptable design within an agreed budget, since the success of these efforts demands consideration and co-ordination of a mass of detail long before the point at which the heating, ventilating, electrical or liftwork subcontractor will be coming along to tell him where his runs of piping and so forth will have to be fitted-in.

If the different design approaches of architect and engineer are to be resolved successfully, it follows that there has to be a good deal of common ground and mutual trust.

Reading between the lines of Spinlove's final letter, he suspects that Thomson Richards and Harriman will probably come up, at the last minute, with a specification for absolutely foolproof Rolls-Royce equipment which will have to be paid for by paring-down his own specifications for the building work, to the detriment not only of visual elegance but of such mundane factors as long-term maintenance – not to mention his own reputation as an architect dedicated to the pursuit of excellence.

His only course, short of a downright rejection (which for reasons already noted, is not really open to him) is to appeal to the bureaucrat in Parbuckle, by suggesting that it would look better if the directors went for the "whiter-than-white" approach of choosing from a short-list of three. If Parbuckle has any sense, he will ask Spinlove to propose the other two, and, with luck, Spinlove will get a consultant of his own choice. If not, he will surely have, at least, the opportunity of discussing the matter and whatever emerges from that discussion will leave him no worse off.

Letter XX: Who Needs Enemies?

Spinlove had better watch it. His irascibility could lead him into making an enemy just where and when he least needs one.

He seems to have deduced from the "Alphonse" that Parbuckle's mother was French. The girth alluded to in the nickname may well indicate that Alphonse was indoctrinated at mama's knee with the respect for good eating which characterizes the citizens of that great republic. The same influence may have inculcated that reverence for protocol which is the hallmark of the *petit fonctionnaire* and which is now being deployed in Spinlove's direction. If so, the latter would do well to observe that food and protocol may be sacred subjects in Alphonse's eyes and, as such, not suitable subjects for levity, especially of that peculiarly xenophobic variety to which Spinlove is prone.

There is, of course, nothing sinister about a client who makes a formal list of requirements even when, as in this case, some of them – such as the bullet-resistant glass – are produced rather early in the day: better too early than too late. Probably what has got up Spinlove's nose is the demand to "acknowledge receipt" of the list as though he, a professional man, could not be trusted to receive it, read it, discuss it and act upon it without more ado. Would Parbuckle have made a similar demand upon his lawyer or his doctor? Well, maybe he would.

In any event, he has rather boxed himself into a corner with his demand for compliance with a British Standard which, almost certainly, he has never read. There is a regrettable tendency, even among people more highly-educated than Parbuckle, to invoke the magic words "all in accordance with B.S. So-and-so" as a kind of *mantra* which will fend-off the evil demon of litigation in the event of trouble. In point of fact, the British Standards which impinge upon the building industry are more in sheer number that any architect or site inspector can possibly have at his fingertips and are liable to revision at such frequent intervals that the description "Standard" tends to lose real significance. More important, a Standard often embodies options – as this one does – and the specifier's choice among these options has to be spelt out with some care if he wants his requirements to be interpreted properly.

Parbuckle has covered *himself* by using an almost meaningless form of words which leaves Spinlove with the baby to hold. Spinlove sees what he is at and doesn't like it. It would have been better for Parbuckle to have said "We want the kind of glass which will protect our cashiers against villains with guns" and left it to the architect to find the best available product through consultation with manufacturers – which is what he will do anyway. As it is, we have the makings of a pretty tetchy relationship. However, Spinlove finished-up on the best of terms with Sir Midas and maybe a few gourmet lunches with Fatso will take care of this situation also.

Letter XXI: Northward Ho!

The episode of the overdue fee (Letter VI) seems to have left no ill-will. Quite the reverse: Spinlove has earned McGurk's respect, on the principle that "a man who can't look after his own money isn't fit to take care of mine". All Spinlove has to do now is to suppress the urge to take the mickey out of people whose attitudes and background he imperfectly comprehends: he nearly made this mistake with Sir Midas and with Parbuckle.

To start with, it is hardly for the bibulous celebrant at the *Reine Pedauque* (Letter XVII) to throw the first stone at somebody who has put away a drop too much on the strength of a pools win (you or I, dear reader, would have ticked the "no publicity" box and avoided the photograph and the begging letters) which exceeded his wildest hopes. And Spinlove should certainly get ready to suppress all those jokey references to blue-painted Picts, sporrans, brochs and Irn-Bru: if they leaked out in conversation, never mind correspondence, he could lose this client.

There is a kind of self-mocking jocularity which serves upwardly-mobile people as a protective screen for their own sensitivities and aspirations. Used-car dealers employ it frequently and so do expatriate Scotsmen: Caliban McGurk happens to be both. It is prudent to consider it as the smile on the face of the tiger: Spinlove may have persuaded himself (wrongly) that it is this client's preferred mode of friendly communication, but if he imagines that McGurk sees himself as a Billy Connolly lookalike – especially with three-quarters of a million under his belt – he could be in for a surprise.

So far, our architect has managed to keep his schoolboy humour under wraps. One must hope he continues to do so, or there could be blood on the heather up at Drumliedubs.

That being said, the advice he is giving is sound. Many a turret and battlement in many a Scottish glen (nowadays, probably a country-house hotel "with own fishing") bears witness to the nostalgia of a Scottish *entrepreneur*, but money is not what it was and the McGurk jackpot will not build him one of these. He could have quite a decent, biggish house which would not be a blot on the landscape provided his architect has enough sensitivity to distinguish between authentic vernacular and phoney baronial. This is one of the matters which Spinlove will tactfully discuss with him – a much better procedure than crudely deflating the client's dream within the four corners of the letter of acceptance itself.

He will also have to explain the purely practical problems which an architect can encounter when he undertakes work remote from his base. In such a situation he has a duty to point out to his client – before, rather than after, rendering his first fee account – the abnormal expense which that may entail. And when, in addition, the building site lies in a country which – even if not "foreign" in the strict sense – does have a legal system, law courts, building regulations and contractual customs of its own, the risks of disappointment are multiplied. Although these complications are not as great as they would be if Spinlove were asked to operate in territory wholly outside the United Kingdom, it is as well that he should recognise their existence in advance.

It would indeed be prudent of him to ask the Royal Incorporation of Architects in Scotland to find a sympathetic collaborator. He would discover that the members of that organisation, so far from being painted blue, are quite as well qualified as himself, having acquired membership on the basis of criteria at least as demanding as these of the Royal Institute of British Architects – to which, in fact, most of them also belong.

The letter eventually sent is not one of Spinlove's best but it deals fairly competently with a situation which is quite new to him and whose pitfalls, although he senses them only vaguely, are not the less real. The term "taking instructions" in his last paragraph is a time-hallowed phrase but Spinlove is probably hoping desperately that the "instructions" will not take the form of a miscellany of mutually-incompatible requirements to which the designer will be expected to adhere in slavish detail, even against his own professional judgement. He will rely on his practised skill to bring out first, in his discussions with the McGurks, the extent of the accommodation they want and can afford – the "etceteras" being examined after, and only after, some sensible first thoughts on this essential precondition of the planning process have emerged.

One hopes that Spinlove obtained friendly and helpful advice on his northward foray and that the commission was brought to a successful conclusion. But this last document exhausts the package of holograph drafts which he laid aside in this particular tin box: and with it the amount of investigative time and energy which the present editor feels able to devote to the exhumation of the Spinlove archives.

AFTERTHOUGHT

I hope that none of my readers will be encouraged to use any of the foregoing letters as a ready-made *pro forma* which can be taken off the peg and run through the copier. The true art of letter writing lies in tuning the message to the occasion, and to the individual who will be reading it.

This is not to deny that the *pro forma* has its proper and useful place in the machinery of communication, but it should not pretend to be a real letter. You are entitled to feel that your intelligence has been insulted when some huckster sends you a "personalised" mailshot complete with the company chairman's facsimile signature in green ink. Consequently that tactic can backfire.

As it did in the case of the traveller who found a flea in his first-class berth on the long haul across the USA, in the days when railroads were railroads. He sent its corpse to the company's President along with a bitterly-worded complaint and got back a deckle-edged and personalised letter to the effect that never before in the railroad's history had a hardship of this kind been inflicted on any passenger on any journey whatsoever and that every conceivable precaution was being taken to ensure that no way would anything like this ever occur in the future.

He might have believed it, except that it came with his own letter clipped on, in the margin of which someone had red-pencilled the simple instruction:

SEND THIS SONOFABITCH THE BUG LETTER

There is a lesson there for all of us.